TEN SHORT LECTURES

ADDRESSED TO THE BOYS

In the Reformatory School

AT HAWDREF GANOL, NEAR NEATH.

BY

JOHN COKE FOWLER, Esq.,

BARRISTER-AT-LAW, AND STIPENDIARY MAGISTRATE,

Chairman of the Managing Committee.

LONDON:
LONGMAN, GREEN, LONGMAN, ROBERTS, & GREEN.
THOMAS THOMAS, NEATH.

PRICE ONE SHILLING.

TO THE REV. SYDNEY TURNER, M.A.,

H.M. Inspector of Reformatory Schools,

THE FOLLOWING ADDRESSES ARE INSCRIBED

IN ACKNOWLEDGMENT OF HIS EMINENT SERVICES

IN THE ORGANIZATION OF REFORMATORY SCHOOLS,

AND OF THE BENEFITS RECEIVED

FROM HIS EXPERIENCE AND COUNSEL

BY THE SCHOOL AT HAWDREF GANOL.

INTRODUCTION.

These short addresses have been composed for the purpose of giving a little advice and information on several interesting subjects to the boys in the Reformatory School, at Hawdref Ganol, in the County of Glamorgan. They are printed precisely as they were written, but in reading them I have found that the attention of the boys is awakened and kept up by occasionally altering the sentences into an interrogative form and pausing for a reply. The School is situated in an isolated spot on the side of a wild Welsh mountain, and visitors rarely approach it. In schools more favourably situated the boys, doubtless, receive much good advice from the neighbouring gentry in addition to the ordinary school-lessons. My object in reading these short papers has been to make up in some measure for the paucity of visitors which our isolated situation has caused. Two of them contain a short sketch of the Christian religion in harmony with the teaching of our Church, and the rest consist of advice and information on various subjects conveyed in the plainest Saxon words that occurred to my mind. The brevity of the sentences. and the extreme homeliness of the phraseology must be attributed to design and not to negligence. In truth, one of my chief inducements to begin these papers was the difficulty of finding anything of the kind that would not be above the comprehension of the majority of such boys as they are intended for. The lecture on cleanliness and ventilation is founded upon two excellent papers for which I am indebted to an accomplished medical friend at Merthyr, T. J. Dyke, Esq. They are, I think, more suitable for circulation amongst adults than very ignorant boys. I hope they will be published for that purpose. Some persons may, perhaps, be of opinion that I have given too much prominence to worldly and secondary motives. I can only say that, without ignoring the power of religion, I have also attempted to work upon the many other motives which, sometimes combined with religion, and sometimes without it, do practically influence the rogue to become an honest member of society.

J. C. F.

The Gnoll, Neath,
1865.

LECTURE I.

What does a Reformatory School mean?

BOYS! This is the first of a few short papers that I mean to read to you about yourselves, and the school, and your way of living after you leave school. The first thing that a boy should get clearly into his head after he comes here is the meaning of the school, and the purpose for which he was sent. You know very well that you have each done something very wrong. You have broken one of the great laws of the land. I cannot tell how often you have done this. But I know that once, at least, you were taken up by a constable, and tried in some Court to see if what the prosecutor said was true. You were found out, convicted, and sent first to prison, and afterwards to this Reformatory School. I do not go back to these things to vex you, but I cannot show you what this school means without bringing to your minds the wrong that you have done. I do not know the particular history of each one of you before you were tried. But I do know the history of some boys of your sort, and I will read to you what one boy has told about his own life. William Thompson said "At the age of fourteen I was sent to the "factory. At length I went strolling about the railway, instead "of looking for work, watching the trains come in, very often "getting three or four jobs in a day, and receiving from 3d. to "6d. for each parcel. I soon spent it, went home and told my "mother I had been looking for work all day. If my mother "said anything to me I would run away from home, and not show "my face for a week. Then I had lodgings to pay and food to "find; how I was to do it I did not know; my mind was not "given to work. I met a companion of mine, he showed me "some money, I asked him where he got it? He said he had "picked a lady's pocket in St. Ann's Square; I thought it very "clever, so we went and got something to eat, paid our lodgings, "and went to bed, and I got into bad company from that time. "Thus we went on for a long time, one thing led to another; at "length the police knew me quite well from seeing me among "bad characters. At last I and another were apprehended in the "Square and sent to Salford prison for a month."

Now I stop here to ask you all this question. Would it not have been a blessing and a mercy to that poor boy if he had then been stopped in his course of crime? You say it would. I will go on with his history. "I was again taken up and sentenced to "two months imprisonment. When my time was up I soon "forgot all my good resolutions I had formed during my impri- "sonment. I was soon taken again for the same offence and got "two months; when the time expired my mother met me at the "gate and tried to get me to go to work but I would not go. I "again took to my former wicked life and went on worse than "before."

This boy was tried and convicted again and again, and at last was transported beyond the seas.

Does your conscience tell any of you that the history of this lad is not very unlike your own? It is very likely that it does. Some years ago you would perhaps have lived the same sort of life for a long time and have been sent at last to penal servitude. But some good and kind people in France and England thought of another way of dealing with bad boys. They saw plainly that though young children are often naughty, yet good teaching and training, and good advice, and kindness, generally make them better. They saw that young animals can be taught to obey in all things those who teach and train them. And they also observed that the young twigs and branches of a tree can be trained up or down, and right or left, at the will of the gardener. But they likewise saw that the tough old branches cannot be bent and twisted like the young ones. These good people believed that bad boys also might by good training be got out of their bad ways into good ways. They believed that if such boys were kept away from their bad companions, and taught to work and read, and kindly treated, they would some day feel a real desire to lead a better life. So they started a few schools to try to do this great benefit to wicked lads. Now after some time it turned out that so many of these boys were ashamed of their bad ways, and turned honest and steady, that the Queen and Parliament took notice of these schools, and thought that more of them ought to be set up. But the Parliament made it a rule that every boy ought to go to a prison for a short time before he goes to a Reformatory School. You have all seen a prison, and you know what it is to spend some time locked up in a cell separately from other prisoners during the long nights. Then from prison you came here. *Now* you are not shut in by walls, and bolts, and bars. You are not separated from your schoolfellows. You have plenty to eat, and a master to teach you to read and write. You are treated just like other boys at other schools; with this difference, that you have healthy work to do out of doors in our gardens, besides your learning in-doors. Now all this costs both trouble and money. The Government and many kind people in this county give money that you may be well taken care of and taught. Do you think they would do this unless they thought it would be for your benefit; unless they really wished to do you good? Why should the Government and we who have to do with this school take trouble about you and such as you? We do so for two reasons. First, we wish to draw you from your bad companions, who would have helped to ruin you, and we want to pluck you out of the consuming fire of a life of crime. Secondly, we wish to lessen the number of thefts and other crimes in this Christian country. We believe that one way to do this is to take charge in schools like this of the boys who were living by plunder and enticing others to break the laws. We hope that most of the boys, if not all, who are committed to our care, will be reformed and changed and turn out honest and industrious men. We do not hope for this happy change and reformation without very good reasons for our hopes. There is no doubt but that the greater part of the lads who enter Reformatory Schools are really reformed. Most of you know the Rev. SYDNEY TURNER, the Inspector, who sometimes visits this school. He was once the governor and manager of a very large Reformatory School. He once said that out of 550 lads who had then left his school 320 had gone out to different British colonies, and that 7 out of every 10 had been really reformed, and instead of being wasps they had become bees. "Some," he was thankful to say, "had taken a still higher "position and become earnest and consistent Christians." I will now read you a bit of a letter which he once received from a young man who had been in his school, and had afterwards been five years abroad. It will show how changed a wicked lad may be by being taken away from his bad companions, and sent to a good school. He says "You have no conception how happy I "felt to see S. S. doing so well. All our lads cling to me in their "little troubles, and I think it no more than my duty to give them "fatherly advice, for you thought it no trouble to direct me, and "I thank God for having raised up such a friend as you, for it "was you, through God's blessing, made a man of me both tem-"poral and spiritual." The writer of that letter was settled in one of our North American colonies. Now in the example of this young man you may see the meaning of a Reformatory School. The school did for him what we wish it to do for you.

He *was* a wasp, and he became a bee. He *was* on the side of rogues and wickedness, and he turned round to the side of honest and worthy men. He *was* an enemy to religion and law; he became a Christian and a good subject of the Queen! But you also are cared for just as that boy was. What ought your own conduct to be while you stop here? Will you not act as that boy did? Will you not, in return for the trouble and money spent upon you, do your best to work with us in all we give you to do? I hope you will try hard to learn to read and write and sum. Such learning will fit you for getting an honest living in ways and places that a poor ignorant lad will not do for. Try also to take pleasure in sowing, and growing, and gathering, our garden crops, watch the animals, learn their habits, be kind to them, and they will soon reward you by knowing your voice and showing pleasure when you are near. If you take an interest in these things your time will pass away both pleasantly and usefully. Fix your minds on the purpose of leaving the school with better desires and hopes than when you came to it. If you have good honest parents or relations, think of the pleasure it will be to them to see you changed for the better. If you have bad relations, consider what a mercy it is that God has given you here a chance of getting out of the way of their example. If you have had little brothers who have seen your bad doings at home, I beg you to repent of having led them astray. If you have set a bad example to any younger boys, then show that you are truly sorry for the mischief you have done. Show it by trying to gain such good habits here as may enable you to make up a little for the evil example you *did* set by the better example you will set when you leave school. Most of you, I hope, look back with shame on the days that are past. Perhaps one or two may think they were happier than they are now. They are mistaken. They may have been more jolly and thoughtless, but not more happy. A mean, sneaking boy, who picks and pilfers cannot be happy. Happiness is some-

thing better than that. There is a conscience in him which tells him he is doing wrong, and his heart is not light within him. God has so made us that we cannot be really happy unless we have a respectable character, and a conscience free from the burden of crimes. I counsel you, therefore, to look forward to enjoy the happiness of possessing a good character, founded upon good conduct and honest intentions. "A good name" says King Solomon "is rather to be chosen than great riches, "and loving favour rather than silver and gold."

LECTURE II.

Truth, Honesty, and Character.

BOYS! Need I ask you what is meant by speaking the truth? If you thought about it you would answer that he who speaks the truth says that which he knows, or what he honestly believes. He who tells a lie states something which he neither knows nor believes. For example, if I say to your Master, "Are all your boys now in this room?" He looks round, counts heads, and says yes or no as the case may be, according to his knowledge. That is the actual truth. If I say to a boy who has just come in from tending the stock, "Are all the cows and horses safe in the pasture?" He says "Yes they are Sir." For having just left them there in safety he honestly believes what he tells me, though he cannot see them.

Why should people ever tell lies? It is not more pleasant to tell a lie than to tell the truth, is it? Certainly not. But if you consider a little, you will find that people generally tell lies for two reasons. First, and commonly, they tell lies because they are cowards in their hearts, and they think that if they tell the truth they will get some blame or punishment for something done or left undone. Secondly, people tell lies because they are rogues, and expect that by telling a lie they will gain some advantage for themselves. Thus you perceive that liars are not only mere liars, but for the most part they are either cowards or rogues. Of course I am now speaking only of those persons who are in the *habit* of lying, and who can never be depended on to speak the truth. Perhaps there is not one boy amongst you all who could now put his hand upon his heart and say 'I can honestly declare that I never told a lie.' I fear there are very few persons who could do so. But if a boy generally loves and speaks the truth, I would not count him with the coward-liars nor with the rogue-liars if some sudden alarm has brought a lie to his lips. So also, if he has forgotten the exact truth and gives a wrong answer to a question without caution, he is careless and thoughtless, but not a deliberate liar. The question is, did he do it coolly? Did he intend to lie? Was he sorry for it afterwards, and did he go and tell the party that he had not spoken the exact truth? If so, it is likely that he will not do the same thing again. The real liars are they who always mean to lie whenever it suits their purpose. For example, a horse-jockey who gets up in the morning with the full purpose of telling a string of lies about the horse he is going to sell in the fair is a rogue-liar. The boy who hates and shirks his work and always intends to escape bad marks or punishment by saying that he has done his work—such a boy is a coward-liar. But the boy who either from carelessness or sudden alarm says that which is not true is not a deliberate liar. Nevertheless he should always confess it, and ask to be forgiven for his error.

But perhaps you wish to ask me what is the harm of a lie? Well, there are several reasons why lies should be avoided and truth spoken. First we are taught that "God is Truth." It follows that God loves to see in us a truthful open and brave spirit. All false ways He utterly abhors. The two stories about Gehazi in the 5th chapter of the 2nd Book of Kings, and about Ananias and Sapphira in the Acts of the Apostles will show you how bad a thing is a deliberate cool lie in the sight of God. Another reason why lies are bad is this, that if everybody, or most persons, were to get into a way of lying, business could not go on as it does now. If I were to promise you beef and plum pudding on a certain day, intending all the time to deceive you, and you found me out, would you ever trust me again? If the Master asks one of you "Have you fed the pigs?" and you coolly answer "Yes," to deceive him, but he finds out that you have left them to starve, can he trust you again? No. What then? Why if we cannot trust each other in such things, aye and in all things, we knock down all chance of being happy and comfortable in our work. The master would be always suspecting his servant, and the servant would think his master wanted to cheat him in his wages, and the customer would suspect the tradesman, and so on. Instead of being friends we should feel as if we had enemies all round us. All this would come from a general habit of lying. I advise you therefore to make up your minds to tell the truth through thick and thin, and then you will help to increase the stock of trust and comfort in the world. Above all beware of Perjury, that is, false swearing in a Court of Justice. What is the meaning of the oath taken by witnesses? It is this. They call upon Almighty God to take notice of what they are going to say, and to punish them if they do not speak the truth. Besides this, if you ever stand in a witness box, and feel inclined to say that which is not true, remember that you yourself may some day be convicted upon the evidence of a liar. Think what your feelings will then be. The Judge and Jury *must* go by the evidence. If it were commonly false no man could feel happy, for neither his life nor his property would be safe. There is hardly a more wicked crime than Perjury. Friendship will not excuse it, for though the false witness may help one side he injures the other. Some of you will certainly some day or other be witnesses. I counsel you not to turn aside from truth. Let neither friendship nor promises tempt you, nor threats alarm you. He who calls you as a witness has a sacred right to your true evidence. If you should be in trouble you have the same right to the true evidence of others. Stand up, then, when you are wanted like true and honest Britons, and never throw dirt into the pure stream of Justice.

Let us now speak and think for a minute about honesty and dishonesty. The law of God forbids dishonesty of every kind, and the laws of England punish many dishonest acts. You all like to have your own money and things, and to feel that they are safe. You may like to *give* them away, but you do not like to have them *taken* away from you. Now if there were no honesty, people could never keep what is their own. There would be no property. Would you like such a state of things? Even the robber does not like to be robbed. Nay, it is so unpleasant that I have heard that rogues and thieves who live together are obliged to agree not to rob each other. If no property were safe there would be no industry, for people would not work hard if they could not keep the fruits of work. You see then that if dishonesty were very common we should all be very uneasy and unhappy. Indeed a dishonest rogue is the enemy of mankind, for when robbers are near the whole neighbourhood is made uneasy. Try daily to be perfectly honest in the least things as well as in big things, and you will soon feel a dread of dishonesty in every shape. Then you may be left in a shop full of cakes and sweets, and you will start back from staining your conscience by taking a farthing's worth of anything. There is one kind of dishonesty which is, I am sorry to say, very common. People *find* articles which have been dropped, or left somewhere, and they pocket and take home the things they find. There may be cases where it is impossible to find the owner, but generally it is not only possible but easy. Now if any one knows the owner of a ring or other article which he has found, or if he has the means of finding him out, and does not do so, but keeps the article, he is no better than a thief. In all such cases make haste to restore whatever you find. Another way in which many people behave dishonestly is by getting into debt, that is, by obtaining goods or money when they know there is little or no hope of paying. As long as you have health, and do not take to drinking, you never need get into debt at all. But if you *are* obliged to borrow or buy things on credit, you should fairly tell the people you deal with what your situation is, and let them judge for themselves. And lastly I advise you to take great care to win and then to keep a good character. You are now building up a new character which has been damaged. When you have lived so long in good and honest ways that it may be safely said of you, "he is a lad I can depend upon; he bears a good character;" you will find *that character* better than gold. That character will have been built upon good conduct, which in the Book of Proverbs is called Wisdom. Solomon says "Her ways are ways of pleasantness and all her paths are peace." A good character justly earned will make you respected and valued by other people, and happy in your own minds.

LECTURE III.

Knowledge, Forethought, and Saving.

Boys! When you go away into the wide world you will have to work for your daily food, and clothing and lodging. If you are well and strong you will be able to live by your labour. But you will not be able to get on any higher or further than that unless you can do something more than strong work with your hands. To get on in the world now-a-days you must be able to read and write and keep an account. You will have to deal with shopkeepers. There will be an account of your wages. How many thousands of disputes and quarrels and misfortunes come from the workman's want of a little knowledge of accounts and figures! If you cannot write and do easy sums, how can you be made a clerk or helper in a shop or office, or be made a weigher at a colliery, or a policeman, or a sergeant in the army, or a telegraph clerk, or a farm bailiff, or a railway porter, or scores of other things? These little situations are all within the reach of a steady young man, if he can but read, write, and keep accounts. Now is your time. These are your golden hours when all this may be learnt. These hours for learning may never come again. No quick sharp lad should sit down content with just earning rough food by rough work. He should look to do more than this by the help of his brains. The proverb says, "Knowledge is power." Is it not a sad pity not to use the chance here given you of starting in life not only with strong arms but also with something useful in your heads? The better you can read, write, and sum, the better chance you will have of getting forward in life. Make your hay then while the sun shines. Many a poor boy has risen bit by bit by his own brains and labour until he has become a rich master instead of a workman. It is true that money and power are not worth much for their own sake. But it is right to seek them if we want to raise ourselves and our families above the fear of want and pinching, and to be useful to aged parents or sick relations and so on. Therefore you should begin as soon as possible to keep some small sum out of the allowance you get here and the wages you will get by and bye. Try even a penny to begin with. Then try two-pence, and go on, as you earn more, to sixpence and a shilling a week. If you set aside a shilling a week for one year you will have £2 12s. 0d. at the end of it. In four years you would have, including interest, nearly eleven pounds. Well! there are many little ways of business which may be commenced with eleven pounds. A small market garden may be rented and stocked, or a small inn or a green-grocer's shop may be taken, or a small pony and cart may be bought, or a passage and outfit to America may be secured, or ten pounds may be given to a first rate gardener to teach you the business. These are only examples of the many things that may be done for your good by the help of eleven pounds, and which empty pockets cannot do.

But how are you to take care of your savings? Foolish people sometimes hide money in the roof, or tie it up in an old stocking, or keep it in a drawer, and a thief gets to know of it and takes it. Sometimes they lend it to persons who are never likely to pay it back. Such persons should honestly ask for the *gift* of a sum and not for the *loan* of it. No one who has saved something by hard work to help him on in business or old age should lend it *all*, unless he gets something as security for repayment. Idle people are ready enough to borrow from thrifty neighbours. But it is far better to *give* something to such persons when you think it is your duty to give, than to lend it without any security.

There are two good ways of taking care of any savings you may collect. You may join a club or Friendly Society. In this case you pay so much a week, and after having been a member for a certain time you are entitled to have a weekly allowance from the Club if you are sick or unable to work. This is all very well *if the Club is a good one.* But many of them are not safe. They often promise to pay out more than they can afford to pay, and then they come to a smash, and the members lose all or most of what they have paid in. There is another objection to Clubs. You can never get back in one lump the money you have paid in. But if you put any savings in the Post Office Savings Bank you will have these advantages. First, your money is safe. Secondly, you can get it out when you want it, either in a lump, or bit by bit. Thirdly, you will get some interest or profit upon the money paid in. You may take the word of one who knows life better than you do that there are no other good, convenient, and safe ways of keeping small savings besides these two.

Some will say, how can I save anything? Shall I not want every penny as it comes? I answer, "you will not." Look at the working men. Most of them lay out a good deal on two things which they *can* do without. I mean strong drink and tobacco. I do not say that either beer or tobacco are bad if too much be not taken. But I say that a young fellow *can* do without them if he likes. You will have your choice. If you wish to make your way upwards you will put by the money you would spend on beer and tobacco. You will deny yourself these things during your younger years that you may be able to save something for your own benefit. If once you begin to drink and smoke it is very unlikely you will ever leave off, or ever save much of your earnings. Try to look a little beyond the present day. If you do not care about rising in life, yet at least think of sickness and old age. What will you do when these come upon you, if you have saved nothing to fall back upon? There are only two things to be done. You will have to be a burden upon your children, or upon the Parish. Far pleasanter will you find it to get forward by the help of a good character and a little money saved into some business or situation which will keep you and yours, and enable you to give your children some good schooling. Try also to make some good friends. Try to secure the friendship of your first master, or your clergyman, or any other good man. Show such persons that you look to them for help in your honest endeavours, and you may be sure they will be pleased to help you. Speak to such a friend openly. Do not be shy and timid. Tell him your thoughts freely, and ask his counsel. No gentleman or clergyman will turn away from a lad who tells him that he wants advice how to make his way by fair work.

I will finish by giving you one more bit of advice. When you get to be nineteen or twenty years of age, then beware of girls and sweethearts. To marry very young is often the road to misery. Young fellows can hardly know their own minds. If you are wise you will not think about marrying till you are in some good way of work or business. Gentlemen hardly ever marry before they are set up in life, and have something to keep a wife and children upon. They are thought very silly if they do so. Prudent workmen will act in the same manner. And if you do make up your mind not to marry until you have got something beforehand, then beware of courting and sweet-hearting when you mean nothing by it.

I have now offered you six bits of advice. First, get all the knowledge you can. Put something by, however little, out of your first earnings. Save by means of the Post Office Bank or a good Club. Keep from beer and tobacco until you have saved £10 at least. Begin at once to form these habits, or it is likely you never will begin. Do not think of marrying until you have enough to keep a family comfortably, and never court until you mean to marry.

LECTURE IV.

Religion.—No. 1.

Boys! You often hear of religion, but I do not think you have very clear thoughts about it. I wish to tell you as simply as I can what is meant by religion. The word religion signifies a keeping back or binding down. If I say that a man is religious I mean that he is *kept back* from doing bad things, not by cords or straps, but by knowledge, and thoughts and feelings that he has within him. And bad acts and thoughts are easily known and separated from good acts and good thoughts by the teaching of the Bible and the Church and our own consciences. But if we know what is bad, and that God hates what is bad, how is it that we should ever like to do it? The answer is that we are all born in sin and with a mind that naturally likes many things which God says are sinful. And though we cannot help being so born at first, yet God has ordained that we may be born again of water and the Holy Ghost. Do you remember the place in the Gospel of St. John where our Saviour taught us this doctrine? You do. What were his own words? "Except a man be born of water and of the Spirit he cannot enter into the kingdom of Heaven." Have you and I been born again of water and of the Spirit? If we have been rightly and truly baptized in the name of the Father and of the Son and of the Holy Ghost, we have been born again. Most of you were brought when you were little children to the font and sprinkled with water in the name of the Holy Trinity. But the Catechism teaches that two things are required in those who are baptized. These are repentance and faith. You will wish to ask me how a little child can have repentance and faith? It cannot. But little children are brought to be baptized by their godfathers and godmothers, who in the name of and for the child declare and answer all that the Church requires. They renounce for him all that is bad and wicked, and state that they believe all the articles of the Christian faith and that they will endeavour to obey and follow the Commandments of God. Now these promises of your godfathers and godmothers you will have to take upon yourselves and confirm and renew when the Bishop confirms you. If in that confirmation you honestly take upon yourselves the baptismal promises and declarations, and if as the Catechism says you have repentance and faith, then it may be truly said that you are religious. The old bad nature with which you were born will be mastered and kept under by the help of the Holy Spirit working in your consciences. And though our inclination to sin does not go away altogether, and though we may or may not lead religious lives after we are baptized, yet certainly we all have the help of God's Spirit so to live if we desire it. God calls us to be good and holy at our baptism. If we use the means he has placed before us we shall have power to grow better and better. If we do not lead a religious life it will be our own fault, and not from any want of help and strength from Heaven.

But I said just now that two things are required in the Christian, namely, repentance and faith. I must now try to explain what is meant by these two words;—the most important words and things in the Christian life. For if you have real repentance and true faith, you may be sure that you have religion, and that you will be safe in the last great day of account. First I will speak of repentance. I think I can best explain it by an example. Call to your minds the parable of the Prodigal Son.

He seems to have got amongst idle and wicked people, and to have forgotten his duty, and thought only of riotous pleasure. At last trouble and want came upon him. Then he remembered that he had offended and forgotten a good and kind father. He came to himself, and began to think about his own conduct to his father. "I will arise," he said, "and go to my father and will say unto him, Father I have sinned against Heaven and before thee and am no more worthy to be called thy son, make me as one of thy hired servants." It was not his own trouble and want that he speaks of, but the wrong he had done in forgetting and offending his father by his bad life. And he not only felt what he said but he acted accordingly. He must have been sadly ashamed to go home, and yet he did go home to seek his father. He showed that he was sorry for his bad conduct. He confessed it and begged to be forgiven. Here you see a spendthrift idle riotous youth becoming very sorry for his wicked life, and really wishing to be reformed and pardoned. You know that the father in the parable represents to us Almighty God. Here then you see how ready and willing God is to forgive us when we repent, if our repentance be real honest and true. The father in the parable does not wait till the son arrives—he goes out to meet him on the way and to lead him back to his home. So God deals with us. When we have offended him and gone against our consciences, God sees any early signs of sorrow for our evil conduct. He will most willingly forgive the offences of these who really repent, and ask him to forgive them for the merits of our Lord Jesus Christ. But he will not attend to any *sham* sorrow. He knows all our thoughts and wishes and feelings, and He will only receive those who return to Him in real trouble for their past offences. "Let the wicked forsake his way" says the Prophet Isaiah "and the unrighteous man his thoughts, and let him return unto the Lord and he will have mercy upon him, and to our God and he will abundantly pardon."

I will give you another example. Suppose that one of our boys has done something very wrong, and is found out. He knows he has done wrong, and that he shall be punished for his offence. The master speaks to him about it, and the boy cries and whimpers and begs to be excused, and promises not to do the same thing any more. But if this comes from shame or from fear or from both, it is not real repentance. If however he is sorry for having been guilty of a bad act; if he sees that the act itself is wicked, and displeasing to God; if he feels that God has seen his sin and he wishes from the bottom of his heart that it may be wiped away and remembered no more; then he is really repenting. But the old proverb says, "a burnt child dreads the fire." And St. John the Baptist not only said "Repent ye" but "bring forth fruits meet for (that is, suitable to) repentance." In other words you must conduct yourselves as if you do really repent. If you have been burnt, as it were, by vice and sin and have felt heartily sorry for it, you must try not to meddle with that fire again. Learn by heart this verse of a beautiful hymn—

Lord when we bend before Thy throne
And our confessions pour,
Teach us to feel the sins we own
And hate what we deplore.

LECTURE V.

Religion.—No 2.

Boys! When I last spoke to you about religion I said that we are all born with the seeds of sin in us. The seeds of anger, and lust and malice and hatred and other bad things are in us from our birth. I also told you that Christ declares that we must be born again before we can be real Christians;—that when we are rightly baptized we are born again by water and the Spirit, and that God then gives us power by that new birth to grow in goodness instead of growing in wickedness. Lastly, I said that if you take upon yourselves at your confirmation the promises made in your baptism by your godfathers and godmothers, and repent of what you have done wrong; if you have faith in our Saviour, and intend and try to conduct yourselves well, then you have religion; you are religious boys; and after death you will go to Heaven.

I tried to explain to you the meaning of repentance by the example of the Prodigal Son. But I had not time to say what I wished about faith. What is faith? You say it is another word for belief. Belief in what? It is belief in the gospel, and in a life after this life in which the good will he separated from the bad, and the good made perfectly happy and the bad punished. Our Saviour said, "Repent ye and believe the gospel." And about the last words he said on earth were these, "He that believeth and is baptized shall be saved." So you see that it is necessary to believe the gospel, or good message of our Lord, if we desire to go to Heaven when we die. I have no doubt but that some of you wish to know what this good message is. It is this. When sin first appeared in this world, the death of the body, and punishment after death, followed sin. The Holy Scriptures tell us that "the wages of sin is death." Our Lord Jesus Christ took pity upon sinful men and women and children; He came into the world in the form of a man, and suffered pain, sorrow, insults, and at last a cruel death by crucifixion. This He, the son of God, did that He might obtain pardon for the sins of the whole world from God the Father. The Scripture says again, "God so loved the world that He gave his only begotten son that whosoever believeth in Him should not perish but have everlasting life." The Bible and the Church (whether it be the Church of England or the Roman Catholic Church) teach us that by the blood of Christ, who was innocent of all sin, and by the virtue of his death, our salvation was made sure. In other words, Christ by his death has made peace between God and man, and God has accepted the death of Christ, that is, the death of Him who had never sinned, instead of the death and the punishment of guilty sinners. If we do believe this in our hearts, because the Bible and the Church say so, then God is willing to look upon us as if our sins were taken away and forgiven and forgotten. If you will listen to the service of the Church next Sunday, you will hear these words, "He pardoneth and absolveth all them that truly repent and unfeignedly (that is honestly) believe his Holy Gospel." This is the chief part of the good message which is called the Gospel. But it is not enough to believe this just as we believe that there was a King of England called George the Third, or that beyond the sea there is a land called America. We believe these and thousands of things besides. But that belief has no power over our behaviour from day to day. But do you really believe that after death your bodies will rise again and that there will be a day of judgment? Do you believe that Christ will then separate the good from the bad, and make the good happy, and punish the bad? Do you really believe that Christ is able and willing to save you in that day if you repent and trust in Him? If you do, you will certainly try to do what He wishes, and not to do such things as displease Him. And if you believe that He has done and suffered so much for you, and for your fathers and mothers and all those whom you love, then you will feel grateful and thankful to Him and wish and try to be like Him. You will keep your hands from violence, and put out of your minds all hatred, malice, and wicked intentions, for our Saviour cannot live amongst such evil thoughts. You must also try to imitate and follow his life and his actions. You know a great deal about Him. You know more about Him than about any one whom you have never seen. You have heard that He was always good and pure and true and kind and forgiving to his enemies. If then we wish to live in Heaven with Him we must *wish* and try to act and speak as He did. This following of Christ will show that we have real faith. If we have faith it is impossible that we can like or intend to be wicked. We cannot help wishing to have a share in the happiness and pleasures and joys of those who are saved by Christ. But who are those pleasures for? Not for those who love crimes and sins. Such as these, who get drunk and swear and murder and steal could not live in the presence of our Saviour. *They could have no pleasure there.* The happiness we hope for in his presence after death must be for such only as wish to be like Him whilst they are living here. I do not say that we can be exactly like Him, for He did no sin. But we can pray and wish to be like Him. This will be the best proof we can have that we do possess faith. It is in the wish, the desire, to be good and pious and like our Saviour in our tempers and actions; it is in this wish and in doing our best to act accordingly, that religion chiefly lies. In other words it lies in the good dispositions of our minds. What these good desires and dispositions ought to be you will find very clearly stated by our Lord himself. In his Sermon on the Mount He has told us what kind of conduct He likes. In the 25th Chapter of St. Matthew's Gospel we are told that they who are kind to the hungry or thirsty, or strangers, or naked, or sick, or to those in prison, shall not be forgotten by Him in the day of judgment if their kindness is real kindness and comes from a right feeling. If we follow Christ in doing kind actions, because we believe his words, and wish to do his will, we shall be blessed in that great day. The good dispositions of our hearts are begun in us by the Holy Ghost at our baptism; they are renewed at confirmation; they are strengthened and kept up by saying our prayers; by doing our best to fight against wicked thoughts; by going to Church and attending to the services; by thinking over any good advice we get; by reading the Holy Gospels; and other good books; and by standing boldly and openly on the side of religion, and on the side of truth and honesty and pure clean conduct, both openly and in secret.

LECTURE VI.

Common Things around us.

Boys! I think you would take more interest in your life out of doors if you knew more about the common things that you are accustomed to see. For example, do you know what is the shape of this firm and solid earth upon which you walk and work? You say truly that it is a great globe or ball, in shape somewhat like an orange. Some of you would like to know how this can be proved. You may easily find the proof that the earth is not flat the next time you go down to the sea-shore. Look out from the high ground above the sea at the most distant ships. If on any clear day a ship is coming towards the shore, the first part of her that you will see are the masts and sails. By and bye you will see the lower part also. If a ship is going away from the shore, the hull will go out of sight first and the sails last. This proves that the ship is passing over an inclined, and not over a flat sea. If the sea were quite flat you would keep every part of her, of equal size, in sight, until she vanished away altogether. Another proof that the earth is round and not flat is the possibility of sailing round it. Look at the map of the world on the wall and suppose the ship to set sail from the Island of St. Helena towards the West, or setting sun. You may sail on and on, and pass Cape Horn and come back in a few months to St. Helena from the East or rising sun by the way of the Cape of Good Hope. If the land and the sea were flat this could not possibly be done. The Earth is about 8,000 miles from one side to the other, and about 24,000 miles measured round. So that if you were to walk fast day and night for about three months without stopping, you would walk as far as it would be through a tunnel to the opposite side of the globe. And this great ball of land and sea is held in the air by the mighty power of God whose laws the Earth, and the Sun and Moon and Stars continually obey.

You have now learnt, if you did not know it before, that the world is a round globe. Can you tell me what this round world is doing? It feels firm and steady under our feet, but is it really fixed and steady? You say it turns round, and you are quite right. Learned men found out long ago by hard work and long sums that the earth and some other globes, some bigger and some smaller, move round and round the Sun. To you and me the Sun appears to rise in the morning and drop out of sight in the evening. But this is not really so. The Sun never moves away from the place where God has put it in the Heavens. The Earth circles round the Sun at a great distance from it. It makes its journey round the Sun in 365 days and nearly six hours. What do you call that number of days and hours? A year; that is to say, the time the Earth takes to make its appointed journey round the Sun. Take a ball or an apple, tie a string to it and whirl it round your head. The Earth and the other planets go round the Sun just as the ball tied to a string flies round your head. But instead of the short distance that the ball flies, the Earth travels in its journey every year a greater distance that we can understand. It travels five hundred millions of miles. You and I are being carried along with it while we are now talking at the rate of more than a thousand miles in every minute. It is hard to belive it. But when you are out of doors on a clear morning or evening, watch the Sun coming in sight, or going out of sight; remember that it is distant ninety-five millions of miles from the Earth; observe the pace at which it seems to rise or drop; and then you will gain some little notion of the pace at which our globe travels.

The Earth has also another movement. It not only makes a yearly journey round the Sun, which gives us the different seasons, but it turns upon its own axis once in twenty-four hours. Axis is a hard word. You will understand what it means by pushing a stick through an orange from the stalk to the opposite side of it, and turning the orange round upon the stick. To be sure, there is no stick pushed through the Earth, but yet the Earth turns round as you turn the orange once in twenty-four hours. This movement makes our day and night. One side is lighted up by the Sun, and the other side is in darkness. The reason why days and nights are not always equally long is too hard for you all to understand now, but if any boy wishes to know more about these things we shall be glad to help him. As the Earth is continually turning, so some part of it is continually coming within view of the Sun. That is what we call Sun-rise. It is now about four o'clock in the afternoon, and the Sun is high in the sky. But there are thousands of people who at this moment are looking at the first streaks of the Sun in the early morning, and thousands more who are looking at his last rays in the West. The people in London, are about two hundred miles more to the East than we are. The Earth moves from the West towards the East, and therefore the Londoners catch sight of the Sun about a quarter of an hour before we do. In Paris, which is still more to the East, they see the Sun about half an hour before we do. And the boys in the great Reformatory School in France are now about half an hour nearer to their supper-time than you are. In Australia it is still night, and the Sun has not risen. And all these curious differences come from the daily movement of this globe upon its own axis.

The Moon is another globe, much less than the Earth. It

circles round the Earth in twenty-seven days seven hours and forty-three minutes, and goes along with it in its journey round the Sun. If you could look at her through a strong glass you would find that there are high mountains in the Moon, some of which spout fire and burning stuff. But whether there are people living there, no one has ever yet found out, and I suppose no one will ever know. To us the Moon does not seem to be so necessary as the Sun. But if we knew all that Almighty God knows we should, perhaps, think differently. Those of you who go to sea will find out that the moon has a great deal to do with sailors. Can any boy tell me how this happens? You say truly that the moon is supposed to be the chief cause of the tides, and you know how important tides are to the mariner.

You work most days of the year out of doors, and see plenty of rain and snow and frost and ice. Has it ever entered into the brains of any of you to think what these common things are? What is rain? Nobody answers. Well, it is moisture, that is little atoms of water, drawn up from the earth into the air, where they gather into clouds. The clouds are collections of those vapours from the earth and they float about in the air over our heads. Sometimes they come down very low. I have seen this school and garden in a cloud. When the clouds look very dark and gloomy you may be sure they will soon let down some of the moisture, and it will fall upon the earth as rain. When the air up above is very cold the vapours are frozen, and then they come down to us in snow. The clouds are, indeed, very useful. They act like great watering-pots for the earth, and they shelter the land, and man, and beast, from the burning rays of the summer-sun.

Can you not tell me what frost and ice mean? You say truly that ice is frozen water. We say there is a frost whenever the air is so cold that water turns hard, and is changed into ice. In some parts of the world the air is always so warm that ice is never seen; in others, the rivers, and even the sea, are frozen for four or five months of every year. Thus you see that water is a very curious article. For if there is heat enough it will all fly away into steam, and if the air is cold enough it will turn so solid that you may travel upon it.

There is yet another thing that you feel almost every day of the year. I mean the wind. It is often very rough and strong on the side of this mountain, and you can hardly stand against it. You cannot see it, and yet it takes off your caps, and carries away slates from our roof, and scatters the thatch of our ricks. What is it? The wind is the air moving, and the motion of the air is chiefly caused by heat in various parts of the world. If you ever go down to the bottom of a coal-pit you will see a great fire at the bottom for the purpose of making the wind blow through the workings. Wherever there is a fire there is a draught. In a pit they call it 'ventilation,' or the making of wind to give fresh air to the colliers. So God sends heat into different parts of the earth, and thus ventilates, that is, makes fresh winds to blow over land and sea. This is one of the ways by which God provides for our wants. The wind fills the sails of thousands upon thousands of vessels; it turns the sails of the windmills; it dries the moist earth, and stirs and freshens the air we breathe, and carries away bad vapours.

These are only a few of the common things around us, about which I should like to talk to you. I should like to make you understand the causes of thunder and lightning and the rainbow; the reason why the stone you throw ever falls to the ground; the use of the lever, the pulley, the wedge and the screw. But I have no time for more. I assure you that there is much pleasure to be had in learning the meaning of common things. If any of you were wise enough to take pleasure in collecting all the plants, or all the ferns, that grow on these mountains, or the butterflies and moths and other insects that creep and fly, it would repay your trouble well. We will gladly help any boy who shows any turn for such things. Collections of every kind of natural objects are full of pleasure to the collector. If one boy were to collect the butterflies, another the moths, another the bird's eggs, another the wild plants, another the ferns, and another the beetles, that are to be found about here, you would gain both treasures and pleasures.

LECTURE VII.

The Farm and the Garden.

Boys! You go out every day to work on our land or in our garden, and it will be useful and pleasant for you to know some reasons for the things you do. But I would rather hear the reasons from you in your own words, if you know them, than tell them to you myself. To begin, then, what is the use of digging the ground as you do? Why would it not do just as well to hoe down the weeds, and rake the ground smooth, and sow it? (Pause.) You answer that the seeds would not grow so well as they would in well dug soil. That is quite true. But then comes the question, why will they not grow so well? The reason is this, that God has ordered that when a seed is put into proper ground it soon begins to swell. After it has swelled a little the part called the 'eye' of the seed is broken, and a fibre or thread is sent out at the opening. This quickly divides into two, and one thread goes downwards, and the other goes upwards. You can tell me what each of these is meant for? The one that goes down forms the root, and the one that goes upwards forms the stem of the plant. Now the root has two uses. First it fixes the plant firmly in its place, so that the wind shall not blow it down; and, secondly, it draws up food out of the soil for the plant to live upon. Take any root of any cabbage or other plant and look at it carefully. You will see that there are thin hairs or spongy points sticking out from the main root, which suck up from the soil the stuff that the plant likes for its food. Thus you see that the vegetables we grow in our garden take in food in almost the same way that you and I take ours, and if they do not get it they fade away and die. They take in from the soil not only water, but certain things called salts and earths which are found in the soils of our earth. Now you will understand why we are obliged to dig our ground before we can sow it. For in the first place you must give the little seed a chance of making the soft fine shoots upwards and downwards in the soil; and next, as all this eating and drinking of the plant goes on underground you must give it room and liberty to feed. If the seed is in prison, as it were; that is if the soil all round it is tight and hard; it cannot make its root and stem as it ought. The air cannot get into the ground to make the food for the mouths of the plant, and the water from the top cannot filter in to mix with the dry food and make it nice and thin for the plant to swallow. You dig the ground, therefore, to open it and bring it as nearly as possible to a powder; so that the seeds and plants may move freely, and also to let in air and water to feed them as they grow. If this is not done; if you drop your seeds among hard clods of clay, or in soil that has been trodden down and is tightly bound together, you must not expect that seeds will do well.

I will only add that when the food and moisture have been sucked in by the roots of the plant, these supplies find their way by little tubes or pipes through the stem up to the head and leaves. This is called the sap. It is the blood and life of the plant or tree. Take a fern or a turnip and cut through the stem in the summer and you will see the juice or sap quite plainly. In the dandelion it will run out like milk on your hand.

You must bear in mind that all I have said about digging is just as true about ploughing. The plough and the harrow are only used instead of the spade, fork, and rake, to loosen and powder the soil of whole fields. There are not labourers enough to *dig* the fields at the right time, and so the farmer gets horses and machines to do it instead of men.

I come now to speak of the use of the manure. Can any boy answer this question? Why, and for what purpose do we mix lime and dung and other manures with the soil? Well! It is hardly fair to expect the answer that I want. I must answer it for you. When you want to raise a cabbage you put a very small seed into your garden. The plant comes up, and in a few months you cut a great heavy cabbage larger than your head. Two or three boiled cabbages make a good dish for dinner. But where does all this good stuff come from. "Out of the soil," you say. Quite true. The soil fed the seed and the plant, till it grew ripe and ready for boiling. There was cabbage-food in the soil. But that food was sucked up all round the cabbage and the soil was left with much less cabbage-food in it than it had before you grew your cabbage. And if you were to sow and grow a cabbage on that very spot for several years together you would find that there was no cabbage-food left in that square foot of ground. Your cabbages would have eaten and drank it all. You would find that the cabbages would get smaller and poorer, and at last would come to nothing worth cutting. It is true that the soil would to our eyes look just the same as ever. But those bits and grains in it which the cabbage likes and lives upon would have been taken out of it. It is just as if you or I should some day be out at sea in a ship with plenty of sand and coal and iron in the hold, and also some water, biscuits, potatoes, pork, and beef, and nothing else. We finish the biscuits, potatoes, pork, beef and water before we come to the end of the voyage. What are we to do then? Shall we try the sand, the coal, or the iron? No; those articles will not keep life in us. If we can get nothing else we shall soon look very queer, and grow very weak, and die. So it is with a plant. There are some kinds of salts and lime which are quite as necessary for the food of our garden vegetables and crops of corn, as meat and bread are for you and me. If you use up all those things in the soil by crops, one after the other, your plants will no more live on the other things in it than you and I could live on the coal and iron in the ship. Here we come to see the use of manure. Dung, and ashes, and lime, and ground bones and other things are used by farmers and gardeners to make up to the soil for the loss of the mineral food it has given to the plants. You must give back by some manure or another the good things which the plants have sucked up. Neither the air nor the rain, nor the digging, will give back these things to the ground. Therefore when you help in the spring to wheel manure to our market garden, bear it in mind that you are carrying food for the new seeds and plants, because those which grew in the same place last year sucked up too much of the good things in the soil to leave enough for another good crop. It is also useful to know that some plants want different food from that of others. And soils differ very much as to the kinds and quantities of salts and lime that they contain. But the principal things in the soil of England and Wales are flint, clay, lime, and iron, in various proportions, and these same things are to be found in the ashes of most plants. Different manures will suit different soils. For example lime is most suitable to the black peaty or boggy land which lies below your school. But I cannot now tell you how to choose manures. You will learn that from your masters and from the experience of other people. Of this, however, you may be sure, that good rotten stable-manure, made of rotten straw and dung, is always good for gardens, and a little quick-lime is also sure to be useful in most places.

Now what I have said so far is true about all land and all gardens.

There is another thing that is only to be done in *some* gardens and fields, and need not be done in others. What is that work? You say it is draining. You are quite right. In a great deal of land in our country, and particularly in Wales, there is too much moisture and water. The first thing to be done is to get rid of that water. There are springs in the land which make large wet places and even bogs, and the rain water lies upon clayey land and will not run off. Why is it necessary to get rid of so much water? Because a quantity of it lying upon and in the land prevents most useful plants from growing. There are plants and animals and insects which like watery soils, and even pools of water. But water-lilies and frogs will not sell in the market, and we should never make our rent out of water-cresses. All the plants we grow in a garden and cook for dinner love a soil that is free from standing or running water. All our useful animals, too, like to live and lie and graze upon a dry soil. It is a very fine thing to be able to turn water upon land now and then; but that is a very different thing from letting it be always there. The general rule is that all damp and wet land must be drained. What is the meaning of a drain? Describe one if you can. You say quite rightly that it is a narrow trench cut in the ground of any depth you like to make it. There are various ways of draining in different parts of the country. Indeed it matters very little how the drains are made if they only make a free outlet for the springs and the top waters. When we only care to carry off the water that lies on the top of the land, it may be done by open shallow trenches. This is called "surface-draining." But when the water has run through the tough soil underneath, then we cut through that tough clay or whatever it is, and collect the water into a deep trench. This is called under-draining. Drains of this kind must be nearly three feet deep. Sometimes they are filled with rubble or broken stones to the height of a foot from the bottom, and then filled up with soil. Sometimes pipes are laid all along the bottom, and protected by tiles laid over them. Of course these drains must have a little fall so that the water collected in them may run towards some big drain. The main drain should run along the lowest part of the land, and pour out its waters into some brook or other water-course. If the small drains are near enough, and deep enough, and well made, the land will soon be left dry, and will be fit for growing the crops. I have now finished my talk about the three great works of farming and gardening. In some places the land is so light and dry that no drains are wanted. But here you may learn not only how to work and manure a garden, and also the great use of drains. On the other side of the valley the drains have been cut and are ready to be filled in. You can see that the land in which they are cut is no longer wet and boggy, while the next piece which has not been drained is a bog in which the snipes still love to feed. If ever you hold land or gardens, keep it in mind that they will not pay you unless you dig or plough well, manure well, and drain well in all wet places.

LECTURE VIII.

General Conduct.

Boys! You have to live together here, and when you go away, you will live with other people. The pleasure and happiness of life depend very much, as you will find, upon the way you behave to others, and the way others behave to you. There is one fine old rule which points out how to behave to other people. That rule is to do to others as we would like others to do to us. It is written in the Gospel of St. Matthew in these words, "Whatsoever ye would that men should do unto you do ye even so to them." It is such a good rule for all people at all times that it is sometimes called "the golden rule." If we did but obey this one rule we should be sure to do our duty to other people. Do you ask me how you are to obey this rule? I answer by trying to think of yourselves as if you were the other person with whom you have something to do. Consider what sort of manners and behaviour and actions, or what kind words or deeds or favours, you would yourselves look for and like, if you were that other person. You are now at school. The only persons with whom you have to do are the Superintendent and his wife and the Assistant Master and your school-fellows. Now if you all kept the golden rule in your thoughts you would be a very happy lot of fellows. If you feel inclined to be idle and careless and troublesome the golden rule would say, "how should I like this if I were teacher instead of scholar?" Is a boy tiresome and thoughtless about spoiling his clothes, or making the bread, or feeding the cattle? The golden rule says, you should not act in that way, for if you yourself had the charge of these things you would be vexed by such conduct. Again; do you like to bully a fresh boy, or tease and make fun of a weaker and slower boy than yourself? The rule says "Behave to your little school-fellows as you would have liked big lads to behave to you when you were small." By and bye you will go out into the wide world and see many more people. The golden rule will then be as good as ever. You will always have to work in order to get your living honestly. Therefore you will always be under the orders of some person who will be over you. How many workmen forget the golden rule! They are so mean that they will work well when the master is in sight, and loiter and waste time when his back is turned. You, I hope, will say to yourselves in such a case, "If "I were a master I should think it very hard and wrong if my "servant or workman cheated me of the time he ought to have "been working. I see that I should be troubled and injured in "my business by such conduct if I myself were master, and "therefore I will not so behave as a workman or a servant. No; "I will not be unfaithful nor impertinent, nor will I waste my "master's time or goods. I will remember the rule, Do to others "as you would wish to be done by." This is indeed a rule of justice. You all wish for justice. You think yourselves badly used if you do not get justice. Be, then, just to others in whatever situation you may be. Sometimes you will be found fault with. You will feel angry and think you are wronged. At such times you must turn over in your minds this question; if I were in his place should not I have found fault just as much as he did? Of course we ought to do this because our Lord has told us so to act. But, besides, you may depend upon it that to be just and fair and reasonable, and quiet, is not only to feel happy ourselves, but helps to make others happy also. Such conduct agrees with the will of God who is just, kind, and merciful, and it goes a long way towards making life pleasant. Just consider what a different sort of world it would be if we were all behaving as the golden rule ordains. If buyers and sellers would put themselves in the place of each other, there would be no more tricks and over-reaching in trade. If masters would always make fair allowance for servants, and servants would think kindly of their masters; if children and boys would think of the pain it must give to a parent to see his child go wrong—if people would call to mind when they quarrel how much provocation they themselves are giving; oh! how much sweeter and pleasanter our lives would be!

I have now given you a few words of advice about your behaviour to other people. I have a few more words to say about some things which I hope you will never do. First, I hope you will keep from swearing both here in our school, and afterwards when you are your own masters. You must confess that it is a very bad habit. Profane swearing is forbidden by the law of God, and also by the law of England. Yet swearing is very common amongst working men. Perhaps you would like to ask me "what is the harm of swearing?" You know very well that there are two kinds of swearing. Some people who swear are in the habit of using the name of God himself profanely and wickedly. This must be very wrong. The name of Him who made us, and by whose will and pleasure we live and breathe, should not be lightly spoken. To sport with his great name shows that we neither love nor fear Him. But how much more wicked is the tongue that calls upon God, the most merciful and most mighty, to curse some person or some creature. There are also other ways of swearing which do not touch or bring in the name of God himself. But a wicked wish is uttered for evil to be done to others; a wish which comes from an angry and spiteful heart. I pray you to keep yourselves from every kind of swearing. It can do you no good. It can only do harm. You may hear people say "It eases my temper, and I cannot help it." That is a poor reason. To knock a man down would often ease an angry temper. Yet men are often very angry, and very seldom knock each other down. Blows do not often follow anger. Why so? Because men know that if they strike blows, they will be pulled up before a magistrate, and so they keep their fists to themselves. This shows that we *can* keep ourselves from violent actions, if we try. So, likewise, we *can* keep ourselves from oaths, curses, and swearing, if we try. To-morrow, perhaps, an oath will come to the tip of your tongue. Perhaps you feel as if you *wanted* to swear. Stop it there, and do not let it pass your lips. The next time you will stop it more easily, and after a time you will feel as if you dared not and could not curse or swear. But if you have ever been used to swearing it will be some time before you feel the same dread of it as if you had never done it at all. Bear it in mind that it is an offence against the law of God; that it is very unpleasant to decent and religious people; that it can do you no good; that it will hurt your character; and lastly that a boy who is constantly swearing is sure by his example to teach others to do the same wrong.

What I have said about swearing is also true about bad language of any sort. You often heard bad words before you came here. I fear that bad words are sometimes heard in this school. Now I ask you what can you possibly gain by bad language? Does dirty or bad language give any one any pleasure? If it does, you may be sure there is something very bad and wrong in that man or boy. Let me tell you that the use of it dirties the minds of those amongst whom it is talked just as mud dirties the clothes. Dirty words come out of a dirty mind. If at any time there are two or three such dirty talkers in the school, put it down amongst yourselves. I do not want you to tell tales about such things, but I do want you to do what you yourselves only *can* do; that is, make it an offence amongst yourselves to curse and swear and use foul language. Never laugh at it. Think of it and speak of it as the custom of blackguards. And when you leave our school bear it in mind that you cannot live with decent people unless you keep a decent tongue. Try to be nice and decent in all your ways. You are in a school in which we hope and pray you will all grow better. I call upon you, and particularly on the oldest boys, to help us in this work. Try to behave in such an obedient, straightforward, trusty and decent manner, that when you leave us you may all be fit to live and talk with honest and decent people.

LECTURE IX.

Cleanliness and Fresh Air.

Boys! It is so good to be clean in our habits that a wise man once said that "cleanliness is next to godliness." Perhaps some dirty fellow will say, "why what is the harm of a little dirt?" I should tell him in the first place, that he will suffer in health. You will easily see how this is when I explain to you what sort of a thing your skin is. The skin covers the outside of our bodies. I suppose you have seen the skin of an ox or a sheep after it has been taken off the carcase. Our skins may be taken off in the same way. One use of the skin of animals and men is to keep the flesh, and blood-vessels and the other inner parts of their bodies tightly bound up together. If you buy some sugar, salt, tea, coffee, mustard, and pepper, at the grocers, he binds them all up a great sheet of brown paper. The skin is to you and me what the brown paper is to all those little articles. It packs and binds us together in a parcel, and prevents us from falling to pieces. Besides this the skin has another use. You know that in hot weather, or after hard work, your skins are covered with a moisture, which you call sweat, and which is also called perspiration. But you must not suppose that it is only in hot weather and after hard work that you perspire or sweat. You are *always* perspiring away though you do not perceive it. I shall astonish you when I say that a man generally sweats moisture from or through his skin to the amount of about two pounds' weight in twenty-four hours, even without hard work. Where does all this moisture come from? It comes from the blood. And what is it made of? It contains a great deal of water, and likewise some bad refuse which the body wants to get rid of. Here we may see how Almighty God has made the skin do useful work for the body. The body sends some of its refuse through the skin, which is pierced by a great number of small pipes called "pores." These pipes carry water and refuse from the inside to the outside of our bodies. They are drains which keep the inside of our bodies fresh and sweet and clean.

You will ask me what has all this to do with cleanliness? Why the refuse which comes through the pipes, or pores, partly flies off into our clothes, and partly sticks to our bodies. Some of it always sticks to the mouth of the pipe or drain, and more or less chokes it. They say that about one hundred grains, or about a quarter of an ounce of this bad stuff comes through our skins in twenty-four hours. If this is allowed to stick to the outside of our bodies and in our clothes much mischief follows. If we are too idle to keep ourselves clean, we must surely pay the penalty for our nasty idleness. For if we are lucky enough to keep our health we become unpleasant to all clean people from the smell of dirt which goes with us wherever we go. Besides this, a great many diseases of the skin, such as itch, ring-worm, sores, &c., &c., are brought on by neglecting to clean the skin. And not only skin diseases, but diseases of the inside, are brought on when the skin cannot do its duty. People with dirty skins are more liable to rheumatism, to catch colds, and to take fevers, than those who keep the skin-drains in good working order. Prevention is better than cure. If illness is likely to come from dirt, what a loss it will be to you to lose the power of earning wages for weeks or months! A good character and good health are the best property of a working man, and he should take good care of both. How much cheaper and nicer it is to take a little extra trouble and spend a penny extra on soap and washing, than to smell of dirt and suffer from sickness! But what is to be done? Why, you have only to wash off the dirt of every day from the outside of your bodies with soap and water, or rub it off by hard rubbing with a rough cloth. In warm weather bathe as often as you can. The teeth also require particular attention. If you are wise you will brush them with soap and water every day. If this is not done you will see an ugly and foul crust grow up all round them. Such a crust is not only nasty to look at, but it brings on decay and pain in the teeth. Many an hour of pain and misery is spent by working men from the neglect of their teeth when they are young. The hair is another thing which wants daily care. Some boys like to wear it long. Nothing can be more foolish. I know nothing that gives a more slovenly and low look to a lad than a quantity of coarse long hair dangling down his face or neck. You never see gentlemen's sons wearing long hair. It is not the fashion. It is very inconvenient for work and for play, and takes much trouble to keep clean. Accustom yourselves to keep your hair reasonably short, like gentlemen; wash it often, and comb it thoroughly with a clean comb twice a day. Take a little honest pride in being clean; in having clean hair, clean feet, clean teeth, and clean skins. Accustom yourselves to cold water, open windows and fresh air, and you will soon discover that you cannot feel comfortable without them. Observe the animals and the birds. How beautifully clean are their bodies and their coats and their feathers, so far as they can reach them with their tongues and beaks. These creatures are taught to love cleanliness by Him who made them. To us he gave the power of thinking, reasoning, and observing, and yet how often we fail to keep ourselves as clean as the bird and the beast!

I will now turn your thoughts for a minute or two to the air we breathe. I am not sure that all of you even know that there is such a thing as the air all round us. Yet we are really living in it, and cannot live without it, just as fish live in the water and cannot live without it. You will hardly believe me when I tell you that the air is now pressing upon every square inch of your bodies and mine with a weight equal to fifteen pounds. You do not feel it in this room. But when the wind blows hard, you feel the air passing by you in a strong current. The air is made of two kinds of gas, called oxygen and hydrogen. There must be certain quantities of each gas in the air we breath. There must be one fifth part of oxygen gas in the air we are to live in. A room that is closely shut, up and full of people, is soon made unfit to live in because there is less oxygen than there ought to be. Every breath we draw in such a room is hurtful to health. If all you forty boys were to sit all day in this school-room with all the doors and windows shut, you would all feel unwell or uncomfortable in the evening. In a small bed-room or any crowded room it is better to put something extra on your bed, or to bear a little cold, for the sake of getting fresh air through an open window. An open chimney or a hole in the ceiling is a great help. Cold fresh air will never hurt you if your clothing is warm, but living and sleeping in close stuffy rooms will certainly do you harm, and may even shorten your lives. Working men often fall into poor health, and sometimes get bad fevers of which they die. They wonder where these troubles come from, and never suspect that they might not have come at all if they had always let plenty of fresh air into their little close rooms every night. I counsel you therefore to keep the room you live and sleep in very clean in every nook and corner. There should be no heaps of dust under the beds. The walls should be whitewashed several times in the year, and especially when there is sickness in the house. Wet clothes should not be hung up to dry in the room you live in, if it is possible to dry them somewhere else. You must get rid of dirty stagnant pools about your dwelling. I have often seen foul heaps of dung and rotten stuff under the very windows of cottages and farm houses. The bad smells that rise from such heaps have often made people sick and ill. The ground which surrounds our houses should be made dry by cutting trenches and filling them with stones, and gutters should be made to carry off waste water, and such things, from the doors.

These bits of advice may seem to you *now* to be worth very little. I do not expect that many of you will remember them. But if a few of the most sensible lads keep in their heads a few of the hints I have here given, they will not be quite thrown away.

LECTURE X.

Life after School.

Boys! This year many of you will leave us and go out into the world to get your own living. I wish you to think a little beforehand about the life you will lead by and bye. My belief is that most of the boys who go out wish in their hearts to lead honest and respectable lives. After having been cut off from your former haunts and companions so long, I am not afraid that you are longing to get back to them. I am only afraid that you may not have strength to stick to your good resolutions. Of course you wish to be happy, and you know in your hearts that you cannot have real peace and happiness unless you are steady and respectable. So I feel pretty sure that you all wish to be steady and respectable young men when you launch out into free life. But there will be many dangers in your path. Some of these I want to point out to you, just as a lighthouse shows dangerous rocks to the mariner at sea. And after pointing to some of these dangerous rocks on which you may make shipwreck in your future life, I will mention some of the best helps for avoiding the danger. The greatest and worst of these dangers is that of falling amongst bad companions. I do not expect that after being so long separated from your old companions in vice you will be in a hurry to *seek* them out again. But it is not unlikely that they may seek you out. For bad fellows are very fond of making others as bad as themselves. And there is many a rogue who will take a devilish sort of pleasure in enticing back a good young fellow, who has turned over a new leaf at a Reformatory School, into mischief and criminal life. Now if any such people do find you out what are you to do? Why! pluck up a good spirit, and tell him, "Dick, I am not "one of your sort now. I wish I never had been, and I never "mean to be again. I have a character to take care of now, "and I am not going to lose it to please you or anybody else. I "know that I once went wrong. But I have had pains taken "with me, and a lot of money spent upon me to make me better. "It was well that I was stopped when I was getting from bad "to worse. Shall I turn against the Queen, and the laws, and "against those who have spoken kindly to me, and against those "who will help me to do well; shall I turn against them, and "above all, shall I go right against my conscience, to please *you*. "Not I." I really believe that many of you will have thoughts like these. Oh, then, if you have such thoughts, take courage; pray for the pluck to speak them out. Never let it be said of you, "Poor fellow, he wished to do well, but alas! his old com- "panion Dick got hold of him and dragged him back against "his will into bad courses." You should say as King David did "O let not my heart be inclined to any evil thing; let me not be "occupied in ungodly works with the men that work wickedness, "lest I eat of such things as please them. Let the righteous "rather smite me friendly and reprove me. Keep me from the "snare that they have laid for me and from the traps of the "wicked doers."* Yes! we may well pray to be kept out of the traps of bad young men. The fear of God and the shame of doing wrong soon fly away in the company of blackguards. And if bad men and boys are dangerous companions, bad girls are worse. If once your thoughts and feelings about girls are blackened and stained, your prospect of real peace and happiness

* Psalm 141.

in life is almost over. You must avoid all low-lived and coarse girls. Believe me that there is no sound on earth so horrible as bad language from the lips of a girl. It is the lowest step in low life. There are plenty of good modest girls in the country. These are the only girls who can ever make a young fellow happy. Let it be your hope to be united some day with a girl of this character, who will share with you your pleasures and your pains, and stand by you till death divides you.

Some of you, I grieve to say, will be exposed to another hard trial. I am supposing that you will go away from our school reformed, that is, changed for the better. I fear that some of you will see much evil and misery in your old homes. If you have reason to expect that this will be the case, your best way will be to seek employment in some distant place. We ought to obey our parents in all lawful things. But we are not expected to obey their foolish or unlawful orders. And as soon as a youth can get his living for himself he will do well to leave the house of a parent who is leading a wicked or criminal life.

Another trial and temptation to a youth who can read is the cheapness of bad books. These are like poison to the mind. Pray remember that such books are bad companions carried in the pocket. You will find that they praise bad actions, and bad men, and make light of crimes, and put dirty things into your minds. Books of this sort are to the mind just the same as bad unwholesome victuals to the body. What would happen if we fed you on bad beef and rotten potatoes for a week or two? You say it would make you all ill. Quite true. And if you feed your brains on foul and dirty food—that is upon bad books, your thoughts and feelings will be poisoned and corrupted. Your bodies may be well enough, but your minds will be very ill. You will find that when you have read a bad book you cannot get rid of it out of your head, however much you may wish to do so. It will bubble up in your thoughts, and even in your dreams, and vex you sadly. So if you see them in the market stalls, or the loan of one is offered to you, turn from them as you would from poisonous food, or from the fang of the adder.

The last trial which you are sure to fall in with is the ever open door of the beer-house. There will be light, and fire, and drink, and company, and, sometimes, music, inside that door. If that were all why should you not go in when your day's work is over. Why! is there not company of all sorts there? Are not some of the people come there to drink till they are drunk? When they begin to get drunk do not they talk in a manner that is unfit for decent Christians to sit and hear? Mind, I do not say that you ought never to go to a beer-house. But I do say that those who sit and watch others getting drunk, and listen to and laugh at their oaths and foul words; such people, I say, are very little better than those who so behave. A beer-house was meant to be a house for refreshing ourselves in. When it is turned into a place for lowering men and women down to the level, yes, below the level of the brutes and beasts, the beer-house becomes a hell upon earth.

You will be ready to say, "it will be hard for us to avoid falling into some of these traps." I well know that it is hard. But then there is help to be had in various ways. For example, some of you, surely, will be religious lads. Your consciences will be hard at work, and will tell you what is wrong, and religion will keep you back from doing it. There is no fear that a good religious fellow will slide down hill into the company of rogues and ruffians and bad girls. No! he has made up his mind to take the side of God in the world. He knows that God has plucked him out of the fire of crime and sin. And having once taken the side of all that is good and honest and honourable, a young fellow of that sort is not likely to be again the mean slave of bad companions and their vices.

There are other young fellows who are not exactly religious.

They think very little of the next world, and a great deal of the present one. One cannot feel so sure about *their* conduct. Yet they have the sense to see that if there were no life beyond the present one, they cannot be truly happy and prosperous unless they are steady and respectable in their habits. To both these classes of young fellows I say "Look out for a real honest steady friend." I do not mean by the word friend a mere pleasant companion, who will work, and walk, and smoke, and lark, and chaff, with you. I mean by a friend, a person of your own sort; one who wants to keep in the right road; to whom you can tell anything you wish to tell; who has sense enough, and kindness enough, to give you good advice; and who will stand by you on the side of all that is right against all that is wrong. It is impossible to tell you the value of such a friend. He is beyond all price. But you must take some trouble to find out such an one. Perhaps he will not seek and find you. You may have to seek for him. Solomon says, "A man that hath friends must show himself friendly; and there is a friend that sticketh closer than a brother."—

> "Friends are they who led by reason
> Mark each others' virtuous life,
> Love, confide, suspect no treason,
> Cheer in peace, and aid in strife."

You will also do well to gain the confidence of some good and kind person in a higher rank than yourselves. It will be your own fault if you cannot find such a person. You may feel shy and timid in going to a gentleman to ask for advice or for his help in obtaining a situation. But you must try to master your shyness, and go to him respectfully, but with confidence in his good will. Especially, I advise you to make a friend of your clergyman or your priest. The clergyman of the parish is a shepherd who ought to care for all the sheep of his flock. You have a right to go to him and make known your case, and your difficulties, and ask for his counsel. Wherever you are I recommend you to make acquaintance with your minister, and do not let him lose sight of you.

The last thing I have to speak of is the manner of spending your evenings. This is a difficult matter. The first thing to be done is to get a comfortable lodging, where you can be warm, and dry, and clean, without running off to the beer-house. If you can read, it will cost you less to take a newspaper every day than to go and drink something at an inn. You may also persuade other young fellows to join you in buying books, and read them one after the other. In almost every town you will find some kind of working mens' library in which you can sit and read. There are penny readings, and cheap concerts, ánd sometimes good acting in the theatres. Make a point of going to all these. They are all less costly than beer, and will help to raise you up to love higher and nobler things than coarse talk and bad ale. If you will only try to take an interest in something that you can do in the evening, you will enjoy life much more than you could without it. You may learn to stuff birds, or make collections of plants, or of insects, or grow a few fine plants in pots, and read about them; or learn the games of chess, backgammon, and draughts, or copy drawings, if you have any turn that way. Above all you may easily learn the notes of music, practise singing or playing in your lodgings, and even join a band. I assure you that evenings spent in such pursuits as these will refresh you after work far more than sitting still. And if I can persuade even *one* of you all to try it, I shall not have spoken these words to you in vain.

T. Thomas, Steam Printer, Machine Ruler, &c., Neath.

www.ingramcontent.com/pod-product-compliance
Lightning Source LLC
LaVergne TN
LVHW012000160826
845678LV00002B/640